# Co-Teaching for Administrators

by Dona C. Bauman, Ph.D.,
Barbara A. Conway, Ed.D.,
and Sonya H. Kunkel, Ed.S.

# Co-Teaching for Administrators

Co-Teaching for Administrators
Copyright ©2017 CREC (Capitol Region Education Council)
All Rights Reserved
www.crec.org

# About the Authors

**Dona C. Bauman, Ph.D.**, has been teaching pre-service teachers on the graduate and undergraduate levels for over 20 years. She is currently an Associate Professor of Education at the University of Scranton and regularly presents at national and international conferences on subjects such as co-teaching, inclusionary practices, and sustainability of school change. She is also a pre-service professional developer in the Strategic Instruction Model through the University of Kansas Center for Research and Learning.

Through her experiences teaching graduate students online from around the country she saw the need to write a book for school administrators. She feels it is the school principal that is the key to a successful inclusive school where good co-teaching is taking place.

One of her greatest joys is watching students grow professionally throughout their undergraduate and graduate programs to become great teachers.

**Barbara A. Conway, Ed.D.**, has been a teacher, and a school principal and school district superintendent for 27 of her 41 years in K–12 education where she served in both public and private schools. While in K–12, she instituted programs for PreK which included a home visiting component and also assisted in launching an award winning after-school program for students in Grades K to 6. The program has since grown to include grades 7 and 8 with an emphasis on STEM. For her efforts, she was recognized as a statewide winner by the Pennsylvania Statewide Afterschool Youth Development Network.

She is currently Director of Clinical Practice for graduate students in Educational Administration and Curriculum and Instruction at the University of Scranton, an online program with students from across the world. In this role, she is the evaluating professor for their capstone practicum experiences where her passion for developing strong school leaders is her driving goal. In addition, she teaches graduate continuing education classes at area colleges.

# Co-Teaching for Administrators

**Sonya H. Kunkel, Ed.S.** has more than 30 years of teaching and training experience as a special education teacher and administrator. Sonya advocates for practices that build specially designed instruction for students with disabilities. Sonya has been honored with awards such as "Educator of the Year" and the "Enterprise Award."

For the past 20 years, Sonya has been presenting nationally and providing technical assistance to district to create positive changes in practices for students with disabilities.

Sonya is known as a practical "teacher's teacher". Her highly respected methods have been proven to increase student scores, create value-added services, and promote educational independence for students with disabilities.

# Preface

Administrators need key resources to help them work "smarter and not harder." This text is intended to provide you with just that: a quick and easy reference to creating and maintaining co-teaching practices in your classrooms. Some key items to note:

- Start with good pairings - if teachers volunteer and get along well, you have a good foundation for growing your program.

- Have teachers teach together for an *entire* lesson block from the activation of instruction through the use of anticipatory sets to formal direct instruction, and culminating with a formative assessment.

- Small group instruction will yield better results than whole group instruction: we call this divide and conquer.

- Make sure your co-teachers *have* and *use* their planning time together.

- Focus instruction on skills and concepts and not on curriculum and "answers."

- Encourage teachers to enjoy the process.

- Remember: ***TTT*** – "things take time."

We'd like to thank Tom Sullivan for all of his technical assistance, CREC for encouraging us to create this book, and all of the teachers and students that work hard together. We wish you well with your co-teaching endeavors and encourage you to contact us if you have any questions. Onward!

<u>www.crec.org/co-teaching</u>

# Co-Teaching for Administrators

## Table of Contents

How to Develop a Collaborative Infrastructure.................1

How to Get the Right People on the Bus............................7

   Story of Silver Lane Elementary School..............................15

Determining Best Practices for Students........................17

Scheduling and Other Logistics.........................................23

Classroom Roles....................................................................27

Environment and Physical Arrangement........................33

Planning Instruction and Small, Flexible Groupings.......45

Guiding Evidence-Based Practices and Planning, Assessment, and Progress Monitoring.............................51

Supervision and Evaluation of Co-Teachers....................57

For Consideration.................................................................69

# Co-Teaching for Administrators

# 1

## How to Develop a Collaborative Infrastructure

*"If you don't really know where you're going, you'll wind up somewhere else."*

*– Yogi Berra*

Any discussion involving the full implementation of the Individuals with Disabilities Act (IDEA) in K to 12 schools or the Every Student Succeeds Act (ESSA), recently put into effect, must also take into consideration the very essence of what is required for its success in school settings: namely a strong collaborative environment where administration, faculty, support staff, and even parents work together for the common goal of achieving equal educational opportunities for all students. However, the debate over where and how students with identified disabilities should be educated still goes on years after the passage of this landmark legislation of 1975.

So what happens then when people, namely administrators and teachers, are "forced" to do something they really may not want to do or even more importantly, understand how to do? In this case, we are talking about public schools creating more inclusive environments in Pre K-12 classrooms by bringing necessary supports and services into general education classrooms thereby fulfilling the mandate of considering these classrooms as the placement of first choice for all learners. Often what happened is that many schools initiated "inclusion" (as the term is called) without giving much thought into the "how-to" of the process. General education teachers found themselves with students in their classrooms who needed specially designed instruction and/ or other supports necessary for success but were not given the tools to help students achieve this success. Perhaps it was lack of adequate and focused professional development or the pressure on school districts to institute these inclusive classrooms quickly, but whatever the reasons, without proper planning and professional development, the inclusive classroom model is doomed to fail.

# Co-Teaching for Administrators

## Getting Started

How then do we get started developing a school-wide inclusive program that demonstrates that all students can learn and that all children can learn together in a supportive environment?

The primary question to consider as a school leader is "What do I believe in?" Keyes, Hanley-Maxwell and Capper in their leadership helix, suggest that school leaders must have spiritual belief or the ability to share with colleagues their personal struggles in adopting (in this case) the value of inclusion (Keyes, Hanley-Maxwell, & Capper, 1999, p. 216). Essentially, if you as leader do not believe in the value of creating and maintaining inclusive classroom environments, then your staff cannot be expected to embrace this vision either. As a school leader, you must believe that inclusion is the right thing to do for children. Similarly, Fullan and Quinn offer that school leaders must first understand their own moral purpose to be able to combine their personal values with the moral purpose (Fullan & Quinn, 2016).

Besides having a strong moral purpose and a spiritual belief that inclusion is right for all children, how can a school leader begin the change process that will assist his/her teachers to embrace inclusion as an integral part of the mission of the school and move forward despite obstacles and setbacks which inevitably will occur?

Munk and Dempsey in their book *Leadership Strategies for Successful Schoolwide Inclusion: The STAR Approach*, suggest that leaders start the change process by visualizing what the process will look like for all the stakeholders. In essence:

- The vision becomes the mission and must be obvious to all stakeholders.

- The principal must share his/her vision and invite all to take part.

- The principal must model for all effected what he/she is willing to do to ensure the goal of inclusive school practices is reached.

- The principal must bring together all stakeholders to plan and carry out the vision and mission (Called "pitching the tent")

- The tent must encircle all stakeholders who feel they have a part in developing this process for the school: faculty, parents, staff, administration, students, etc.

- The principal must develop leadership among the stakeholders and recognize when to lead and when to fall back and support (Munk &

# How to Develop a Collaborative Infrastructure

Dempsey, 2010, pp. 40-43)

Munk and Dempsey also state that teachers will resist changes made in school if they do not really know what is expected of them in the change process (Munk & Dempsey, 2010). In other words, they don't have a clear picture of what the initiative looks like when successful. On the positive side, the authors posit that when a diverse group of people come together to develop an inclusive school, it can result in community pride.

Along with the visualization of the actual change process, Fullan and Quinn offer some suggestions to assist school leaders to develop the needed moral purpose in the key stakeholders (Fullan and Quinn, 2016, p. 19).

School leaders:

- Must build relationships with everyone, including those who disagree, are skeptical or even cynical.

- Must listen and understand the perspective of all.

- Must demonstrate respect for all.

- Must create conditions to connect others around the purpose.

- Must examine the staff evidence of progress.

## Moving Forward

In order to move any initiative foreword, steps must be taken. The stakeholders must see action taking place beyond conversations to maintain momentum in this change process. Fullan and Quinn suggest that an action plan with a small number of goals, and a clear systematic plan to achieve these goals and a way to recognize when the goals have been attained, must be developed (Fullan & Quinn, 2016). Celebrations should also be included, as part of this process and of course problem-solving strategies must be implemented when goals are not reached. Muraski and Dieker call this the "no whine" theme (Muraski & Dieker, 2013). The key here is that educators cannot whine when there is a bump in the road but rather they must find a solution or even multiple solutions to address the problems. Successful inclusive schools find solutions to problems!

One of the most important pieces in facilitating the collaborative inclusive community envisioned here is for the school leader to provide his/her faculty with the most precious commodity- time. Time is needed for numerous areas such as: conversations about what is working and what is not, team/grade level meetings, ongoing professional development, visits to other classrooms or schools where inclusive practices can be observed, conferring

# Co-Teaching for Administrators

with parents, support staff, the list goes on and on. What is also essential is that the school leader provides the resources needed for the teacher to be successful in the classroom. A cautionary note: School building leaders should hold conversations with district leaders so that, he/she can be sure of district support, be it financial or staff support, in maintaining and building a successful inclusive school.

## References

Fullan, M., & Quinn, J. (2016). *Coherence: The Right Drivers in Action for Schools, Districts, and Systems*. Thousand Oaks, California: Corwin.

Keyes, M., Maxwell, C., & Capper, C. (1999). *Spirituality? It's the core of my leadership: Empowering leadership in an inclusive elementary school*, Educational Administration Quarterly, 35(2), pp. 203-237.

Munk, D., & Dempsey, T. (2010). *Leadership Strategies for Successful Schoolwide Inclusion*. Paul H. Brooks Publishing Co.

Muraski, W. & Dieker, L. (2013). *Leading the Co-Teaching Dance*. Arlington, Virginia: Council for Exceptional Children.

# Co-Teaching for Administrators

# 2

## How to Get the Right People on the Bus

*Driver: "Hi, I'm the bus driver. I've got to leave for a little while, so can you watch things for me until I get back? Thanks. Oh and remember: Don't let the pigeon drive the bus!"*

*Pigeon: "I thought he'd never leave!"*

*– Mo Willems, "Don't Let the Pigeon Drive the Bus"*

Let's talk about how to begin and bring all the stakeholders onto the bus! Unlike the pigeon, as school leaders, we want everyone on the bus... the question is who will drive the bus and who are the passengers? As the educational leader, it must be made clear to all stakeholders that the development of an inclusive environment for all students is a process that will not happen overnight. Rather it will unfold and progress. Villa and Thousand point out that organizational transformation requires ongoing attention to consensus building for the inclusive vision to be successful (Villa & Thousand, 2003, pp. 19-23).

It is important also that the individual who is initiating the process (the driver) —be it the Superintendent of the district or Director of Special Education- must have a clear picture of what they want to do and how they want to roll out the change. Questions they may need to ask themselves are:

- What do I believe about the ability of all children to learn?

- How can my school/district design a program that will ensure that all children will learn?

- Do I feel that children who have differences really belong in my school and/or district? (This goes to the heart of the "spiritual belief" previously discussed)

# Co-Teaching for Administrators

- Can I provide the best education for all children with the resources I currently have? If not, how can I obtain the needed resources?

- How do I bring all the needed stakeholders "onto the bus" and help them feel that they are part of the change process?

- Who will be the wet blanket and how can I bring them aboard? Are there some who will not be able to come on board?

Once the educational leader (the "driver") has a clear understanding of what his/her belief system is concerning inclusive education, then it is time to bring in others.

The best advice to the "drivers": Start small! The following is a simple example of how to proceed:

- Identify a principal who embraces the belief that all children can learn.

- Meet with the principal and discuss the development of an inclusive environment that supports a co-teaching strategy.

- The principal will then identify key staff members who will be the leadership team in developing and promoting the co-teaching initiative.

- The leadership team will be tasked with the development of an implementation plan which will guide the school in its journey towards an inclusive environment where all children's needs are met.

- The leadership team will help identify faculty members who they feel will be receptive to working toward establishing an inclusive classroom that uses a co-teaching model.

## A note concerning the leadership team

Professional development must be provided to the leadership team as they develop their plan. This may include site visits to schools that are recognized as having successful inclusive environments which feature co-teaching as a strategy. Other professional development opportunities may include: professional conferences, on site professional development using recognized experts in the field or representatives of your state department of education. On- site training may include the use of IRIS Modules from Vanderbilt University. (URL) Finally, if you have a relationship with a nearby institution of higher learning, you may be able to partner with their inclusion specialists.

Remember: One of the goals of starting small is to establish a successful model that can serve as an example in order to expand the initiative. It is

## How to Get the Right People on the Bus

important that the identified faculty members who will serve as co-teachers, will in turn, share their successes with the rest of the school community and outside public.

### Who else can "drive the bus"?

Once the leadership team has determined the faculty members who will serve as the initial "cohort" of co-teachers, Smith, Polloway, Patton & Dowdy suggest the next step is preparing them for their task as co-teachers in an inclusive environment.

Three major training activities are suggested:

- Opportunities to see good examples of inclusion.

- Provision of information about inclusion, student diversity, inclusion related practices, and the development of skills that the teachers need to feel comfortable and competent.

- The time to plan with other team members (Smith, Polloway, Patton, & Dowdy, 2004, p. 57).

### The Passengers?

Thus far we have discussed several steps towards the creation of an inclusive environment that supports co-teaching:

- school leader whose vision is the creation of the initiative,

- the identification of a "small" model program in a setting with a leader who also supports the vison,

- the establishment of a leadership team with identified tasks, and

- the identification of teachers who will implement the vision, in this case, the co-teaching model in a fully supported inclusive environment.

But now what about the "passengers" on the bus? Other teachers not initially involved in the co-teaching initiative- the students, parents, perhaps even community members?

First and foremost, all students must be the primary focus of any educational initiative. Selection of students most likely to succeed in an inclusive co-teaching environment is discussed in the following chapter. Smith et. al. suggest essential features that would benefit all students in an inclusion classroom:

- A sense of community and acceptance, (every student is valued and nurtured)

- An appreciation of student diversity, (recognition and celebration of all types of diversity)

- Attention to all curricular needs, (meaningful content and approaches and materials that work best for all)

- Effective management and instruction,

- Personnel support and collaboration (including para-educators and other service related professionals) (Smith et al., 2004, pp. 37-38.)

As mentioned previously, faculty members who will be co-teaching (and we assume they are willing and anxious to participate in this initiative) must be provided with ongoing professional development which will provide them with the necessary information and continued support to help make their efforts successful. But we must also consider those teachers who are very reluctant to be involved in inclusion and want nothing to do with co-teaching. They are the ones that make statements like:

"This is my classroom." (The message to the special education teacher is sit in the corner and don't move.)

"Well, those children can be in my classroom but they have to keep up with the class."

"It is not fair that I have to make changes in my curriculum or give them advantages that I don't give anyone else."

"You take care of your students (in special education) and I will take care of the rest."

It is important to note that both special education teachers and general education teachers may have negative attitudes towards inclusion and co-teaching. How do you change the attitude of teachers who are very reluctant to try inclusive practices? You need to have patience as this group may be difficult to work with.

Some suggestions to work with this reluctant or even adversarial group are:

- Bring in a speaker who explains special educational law thereby increasing their understanding of their mandate to serve all children (Muraski & Dieker, 2013).

- Listen to and acknowledge their concerns.

## How to Get the Right People on the Bus

- Provide success stories and celebrate those who have chosen to co-teach at a whole school in-service.

- Have successful co-teachers talk about their experiences.

- Send your reluctant participants to conferences or possibly provide a motivational speaker that may inspire them.

- Provide ongoing coaching by an instructional specialist.

The bottom line here is: It may take them some time for the naysayers to become willing participants but don't give up on them. Continual communication is key. As Reginald Green notes "school leaders need to communicate the change initiative (in this case, the development of a co-teaching model in an inclusive setting) by...describing how they (students and to some extent faculty) will benefit when the change initiative is implemented" (Green, 2010, p.185). The bus is leaving and as with any change, there will always be those who are the last ones to board. They may need extra tender, loving care!

Communicating with parents (those who have children with special needs and those whose children do not but are in the "co-teaching" classroom) is another area that will require focus from school leaders. Some suggestions include:

- Provide information on the initiative that is understandable and that emphasizes the positive outcomes expected for all students.

- Invite parents to attend informational meetings where questions can be addressed.

- Form a Parent Advisory Council that will bring concerns to school administration and also celebrate the successes as they occur.

- View parents as partners.

- Use social media such as school/class websites to highlight classroom activities and special events.

- Send out a positive and upbeat letter welcoming students to the class from both teachers.

- Put both teachers names on schedules, communications outside the door, and in all prominent locations.

Parents who support school initiatives do so because they feel as though they are included, informed and valued, and are therefore one of the most powerful tools in "spreading the word" of the good work that is occurring in the school to other parents as well as community members.

## Some Final Thoughts on Collaboration and Problem Solving

Discussion in this chapter focused on "getting the right people on the bus" in establishing and maintaining a successful inclusion model. Yet, even in the most successful schools where collaborative practices are second-nature, problems may arise. The ability to define and solve problems is a definitive characteristic of schools who truly possess a "culture of collaboration". This culture as we have seen, begins with the leader. As Munk and Dempsey point out, the leader, in most cases the principal, must demonstrate that they are role models for the change initiatives they espouse to their faculty, must articulate and initiative change with a clear vision of what the results will look like for all stakeholders, and are able to play the lead role in front of their school teams or lead from the rear while letting others take the lead (Munk & Dempsey, 2010, p. 39).

Additionally, schools with strong collaborative structures also have established effective problem solving skills. Nancy Waldron and James McLeskey offer that when a school has a culture of collaboration, activities such as joint problem solving, data sharing and analysis, shared decision-making, and distributed leadership are present (Waldron & McLeskey, 2010). Further, they posit that these "collaborative activities result in added value by generating multiple solutions to complex problems and provide opportunities to learn from others as school professionals express and share expertise" (Waldron & McLeskey, 2010, p. 59). Finally, they offer that when collaborative efforts take place, the results lead to " higher levels of trust and respect among colleagues, improved professional satisfaction, improved instructional practices, better outcomes for all students..." (Waldron & McLeskey, 2010, p. 59).

**References**

Green, Reginald. (2010). T*he Four Dimensions of Principal Leadership: A Framework for Leading 21st Century Schools.* New York: Allyn & Bacon. p. 185.

Muraski, W. & Dieker, L. (2013). *Leading the Co-Teaching Dance.* Arlington, Virginia: Council for Exceptional Children.

Smith, T., Polloway, E., Patton, J., & Dowdy, C. (2004). *Teaching Students with Special Needs.* New York, New York: Pearson.
p. 57

Villa, R., & Thousand, J. (2003). *Making Inclusive Education Work,* Educational Leadership, 61(2) pp. 19-23.

Waldron, N. & McLeskey, J. (2010). *Establishing a Collaborative School Culture Through Comprehensive School Reform,* Journal of Educational and Psychological Consultation, 20, pp. 58-75.

Willems, Mo. (2003). *Don't Let the Pigeon Drive the Bus.* New York, New York: Hyperion Books for Children,

# Co-Teaching for Administrators

# 2.5

## The Story of Silver Lane School

Chapters 1 and 2 suggested steps in helping to develop a collaborative infrastructure and how to get the right people on the bus in moving toward establishing a viable and vibrant co-teaching model. Perhaps a short story of Silver Lane Elementary School can serve as an example for the principal who needs a little more information and will assist him/ her to move beyond the beginning steps suggested in the opening chapters.

Silver Lane Elementary School under the tutelage of former Principal Catherine Ciccomascola demonstrated a well developed inclusive philosophy and practice that could serve as an example to other schools. Silver Lane Elementary is part of the East Hartford School District in East Hartford, Conn. The mission of the school as stated on their webstie (http://www.easthartford.org/silver-lane-elementary) is: *"Together We're Better."*

The mission of Silver Lane School is to work in partnership to educate all students to their fullest potential. Through high standards and expectations of excellence, the staff is committed to promoting a safe, orderly and caring environment that respects and supports the development of the whole child.

The Silver Lane School enrolls approximately 300 students at the PK-6 grade levels and has a large transient student population, a large majority of whom receive free or reduced lunch. The school uses data-driven decision making to modify instructional processes. The school has a data team that meets regularly and makes recommendations to the district and school board based on evidence from the data. Not only does Silver Lane collect data to make school wide decisions, data is collected to make individual decisions for each child. Teachers also use the data to configure and refigure groups. They could go from whole group instruction to flexible grouping. Silver Lane uses co-teaching extensively with one co-teaching team per grade level. The practice of co-teaching is so ingrained into the school that a power point presentation on co-teaching is part of the school's web page.

# Co-Teaching for Administrators

The following information was collected from a focus group conducted by the authors of this text in December 2012.

The former principal came to the school with experience in special education. She had a strong belief system that supported inclusion in the school with the emphasis on each child being educated to their fullest expectations. Having high expectations for each child was part of the belief system that she brought to the school and expected no less from her staff. If a staff member could not agree with the philosophy it was suggested to that staff member that perhaps they would be happier teaching at another school in the district. This was done with respect for the person with a differing view but there was no room for doubt what was expected from the teacher. School leaders must have the conviction of their beliefs and philosophy and be able to stand up to those who might not have the same beliefs and philosophy. They may want to consider stating that if you can't be a part of this initiative then perhaps you need to move on. A principal has to make the hard decision that this is the way it is going to be.

The former principal quickly established a supportive team of teachers and sent those teachers for professional development in inclusion and co-teaching. The principal has always recognized teacher leadership and provided professional development as well as mentoring to those who she recognized as leaders. She also scheduled planning time for each co-teaching partnership so that they would have the time to plan for instruction. This corps of teachers became the ambassadors for inclusion and co-teaching. She energized the school staff and recognized what the school staff is good at and encouraged them to become even better. The principal recognizes that this collaborative relationship is an extremely important part of inclusion as well as school improvement.

# 3

## Determining Best Practices for Students

*Abbott: I am telling you. Who's on first, What's on second, I Don't Know is on third...*

*Costello: You don't know the fellow's names?*

*Abbott: Yes*

*Costello: Well, then who's playing first*

*Abbott: Yes*

*Costello: I mean the fellow's name on first base.*

*Abbott: Who*

### Who receives co-teaching services?

Co-teaching is a practice used to boost student outcomes. Two professionals contract to share instructional responsibility for the same group of students in the same location, although roles and materials may vary (Friend & Cook, 2000). Teachers' roles should be focused on instructional delivery methods that allow for student success. "Research supports that co-taught classrooms benefit all students (Abdallah, 2009)." Research suggests that students in a co-taught class can out perform students in a solo-taught class (Almon& Feng, 2012). .

We may find all types of professionals invested in collaborative partnerships. Regardless of the pairings and efforts to get the right people on the bus, co-teaching is ultimately about serving the best interest of students. How do we select the students for these classrooms? Who's on first?

# Co-Teaching for Administrators

Here are three major considerations when selecting students for co-teaching:

1. Consider the students' need for specific instructional strategies that are pre-planned (example: similar IEP goals)

    a. To select students in need of instructional practices, take a look at evidence of their specific skill deficits (example: place 4-5 children with needs in developing comprehension strategies together in a classroom)

    b. To select students with a need for strategic practices, look at evidence of intervention needs. Select and group students together with similar profiles or needs for standard treatment protocols (a sequence of three to ten mini-lessons aimed at re-teaching specific skills as measured by brief assessments). Co-teaching may be considered a tier 1 and/or tier 2 practice under a multi-tiered intervention framework.

    c. To select students in need of access as provided by a Universal Design for Learning approach, look for their success when offered practices such as differentiated instruction, or multiple intelligence theories. (example: student is successful when provided with numerous ways to learn vocabulary such as visual representations and kinesthetic strategies at the same time)

2. Consider the students' need for behavioral supports to aid in the integration and normalization of appropriate behaviors (example: embedded practice and generalization of executive function skills)

    a. To select students in need of particular structures or management strategies that will be on-going and built into the particular class, look at the students' success with the type of classroom management system used by the co-teaching pair.

    b. A warning here, placing more than 2 students with significant behavioral support needs in one class could be behaviorally overwhelming for both the students and the teachers.

3. Consider the students' need for social opportunities for skill development and practice (example: opportunities to learn and practice appropriate school and social norms in context)

    a. To select students in need of social opportunities, consider the make-up of the rest of the class. In some situations, it may be best practice to have students in need of social development be placed

# Determining Best Practices for Students

in a class with students with high ability level, or with students with high self-esteem. Classrooms that pool students with lower ability level or low self-esteem offer fewer opportunities to practice appropriate social skills in context due to the lack of appropriate role models.

  b. Select classes where the curriculum is geared towards social opportunities to provide many natural opportunities to practice skills.

What are three considerations for selecting students for other practices (NOT co-teaching)?

1. Support (example: over the shoulder help, reiteration of instructional directions)

   a. Since co-teaching is NOT a support, but an instructional practice, support is best done in classrooms that are staffed with paraeducators. To select a student in need of support, look for students who have consistently demonstrated good effort and fair to average grades/ skill acquisition.

   b. A word of warning about "supported classes" – the potential to create students that are "disengaged" learners is high. Through a support model, students can quickly learn they do not need to engage in learning because the support person will cater to their instructional needs. Professionals sometimes refer to these students as "enabled" students or as students that have "learned helplessness." A highly evolved co-teaching classroom engages all students in the class in flexible small group instruction practices at least 80 percent of the time.

2. Tutorial help (example: re-teaching what was just taught, 1:1) Tutorial help is generally provided by a specialist such as a tutor, an English learners' teacher, and in some cases a therapist with specialized skills sets such as an occupational therapist. Students in need of tutorial support are considered "average to above average" students with a specific need.

   a. Some students in need of extra tutorial support, such as an English Learner, or a student with a recent Traumatic Brain Injury may be good candidates for a tutorial approach.

   b. Due to complicated medical circumstances, a child may need ongoing tutoring to keep them abreast of the curriculum demands. These are students that would typically be successful if not for the

# Co-Teaching for Administrators

      medical condition (example: chronic fatigue syndrome or a student receiving cancer treatments.)

3. Just because the student has an IEP....

   a. Just having an IEP does not mean the student needs co-teaching. Co-teaching should be a service used to work on a student's goals integrated with the general education curriculum. A student with NO math goals would not need co-teaching in math. Or, a student receiving specialized reading instruction in a resource room to meet their decoding goals, wouldn't necessarily need co-teaching for writing.

   b. Co-teaching is part of the continuum of services in special education, but should not be the only practice used to meet students' needs. Students should be selected in a judicious manner after reviewing files and matching the instructional opportunity to their needs.

   c. Universal Design for Learning (UDL) is an important part of co-teaching planning. This approach proactively creates access points in instruction for all learners through a variety of methods

*"To live is to choose. But to choose well, you must know who you are and what you stand for, where you want to go, and why you want to get there."*

*– **Kofi Annon***

**References**

Abdallah, J. (2009). Benefits of Co-teaching for ESL classrooms. Academic Leadership. 7(1)

Almon, S., & Feng, J. (2012). *Co-Teaching vs. Solo-Teaching: Effect on Fourth Graders' Math Achievement.* Lexington, KY

Friend, M., & Cook, L. (2000). *Interactions: Collaboration Skills for School Professionals, 3rd Edition.* New York, New York: Pearson.

# Co-Teaching for Administrators

# 4

## Scheduling and Other Logistics

*Ricky: We'll write down everything you need to do during the day, and we'll allow so much time for each thing. Ten minutes for this, 15 minutes for that...*

*Lucy: Oh, I'm going to need more than 15 minutes for that.*

*– I Love Lucy, Episode 33 "Lucy's Schedule"*

### How do you schedule teachers for co-teaching?

Here are some frequently asked questions about co-teaching schedules:

- How much time should co-teachers teach together?
- How much planning time should be allotted?
- If co-teachers are not together every day, does the inconsistency undermine their parity in the classroom?
- Are there any creative scheduling options?

There are many ways that co-teachers can work together. The most important aspect of the instructional component of the partnership is that when co-teachers are together, both teachers teach to predefined instructional objectives and have clearly defined roles and assessment routines. Administrators want to ensure co-teaching opportunities maximize the available human and tangible resources to boost student outcomes.

The accumulation of experience and research evidence to date strongly indicates that common planning can make a difference in building stable staff that are committed, responsive, and collectively responsible for instructional

# Co-Teaching for Administrators

improvement and student achievement (Legters, Adams, & Williams, 2010).

## Scheduling Practices to Consider

Typical Elementary School Schedule/ Block Schedules:

- Co-teaching should occur so that lessons can be completed by both teachers that include anticipatory sets, instruction, guided practice and assessment. A mistake is often made when the "entering" co-teacher creates a schedule predicated on ½ hour blocks of time. When this is the case, the entering teacher does not have the time to fully participate and provide a teaching cycle as described above.

- It is best to have co-teaching 2-3 times a week for larger blocks of time, than daily co-teaching for small amounts of time. With blocks, teachers will have more options for creating flexible groups, and for offering targeted instruction.

- If you choose to have co-teacher work together 2-3 times a week, consider having the co-teaching days be contiguous and not separated (every other day of example.) Contiguous days allow for completion and follow-through with lessons. Every other day approaches are very difficult to plan, especially when teachers need to adjust lessons based on formative and summative data.

Middle School/High School Schedules with Timed Bells

- There are many versions of school schedules. Consider having co-teachers work together most days, and create some "non-co-teaching" days. This approach will allow you to create planning opportunities if needed. See Table 1 on the next page for an example. In this example, a co-teacher will work with his/her counterpart for 4 out of 5 days. On the 5th day, the co-teacher meets with another teacher for planning (during their scheduled planning time.)

- The contiguous co-teaching days allow for lesson follow-through and multi-day lesson approaches. The planning time (presumably the general education teacher's regularly scheduled planning), creates the collaborative opportunity to prepare the next set of lessons.

# Scheduling and Other Logistics

## Table 1

| Monday | Tuesday | Wednesday | Thursday | Friday |
|---|---|---|---|---|
| Co-teach with Teacher A | Co-teach with Teacher A | Co-teach with Teacher A | Co-teach with Teacher A | Co-PLAN with Teacher B |
| Co-PLAN with Teacher A | Co-teach with Teacher B | Co-teach with Teacher B | Co-teach with Teacher B | Co-teach with Teacher B |

- SCHEDULE PLANNING TIME FIRST, then schedule the co-teaching sections. Quite often, schedules are created by putting in the classes first and then administrators are challenged with trying to manipulate blocks of time to find planning time. By scheduling planning time first, you send a message that planning is THE MOST IMPORTANT aspect of co-teaching. Without planning, you generally end up with a supported class, and not a class whereby professionals offer specially designed instruction.

## Resources

Here are two resources to review when taking scheduling and planning into consideration:

*Finding Time for Common Planning and/or Teacher Collaboration. (Pathway Communities of Practice)*

https://casn.berkeley.edu/resource_files/S1_Finding_Time_Common_Planning_Teacher_Collaboration.pdf

*National School Reform Faculty: Free Activities and Protocols*

https://www.nsrfharmony.org/free-resources/protocols/a-z

*"The key is not to prioritize what's on your schedule, but to schedule your priorities."*

*– Stephen Covey*

## References

Ledgers, N., Adams, D., & Williams, *Common Planning: A Linchpin Practice in Transforming Secondary Schools*. (2010). Academy for Educational Development. Prepared of the United States Department of Education Office of Elementary and Secondary Education. Retrieved from https://www2.ed.gov/programs/slcp/finalcommon.pdf

# 5

## Classroom Roles

*This is a story about four people: Everybody, Somebody, Anybody and Nobody.*

*There was an important job to be done and Everybody was asked to do it.*

*Everybody was sure that Somebody would do it.*

*Anybody could have done it, but Nobody did.*

*Somebody got angry because it was Everybody's job.*

*Everybody knew that Anybody could do it,*

*but Nobody realised that Somebody wouldn't do it.*

*And it ended up that Everybody blamed Somebody*

*because Nobody did what Anybody could have done.*

– **Charles Osgood**, *A Poem About Responsibility*

### What are the roles of two teachers in the co-taught classroom?

First let's look at what Wiggins and McTighe describe as the 3 important components of a teacher's role:

- Didactic/ Direct Instruction (examples: Demonstration/Modeling/ Questioning)

- Facilitation of Understanding (examples: Problem-based learning, Simulation, Experimental Inquiry)

# Co-Teaching for Administrators

- Coaching (examples: Conferencing, Feedback)

- Effective teachers not only demonstrate skills in all three roles, but also understand when they should be used, in what combinations, and for how long. (Wiggins & McTighe, 2007). Therefore, it stands to reason, co-teachers should be maximizing the expertise of two individuals to fulfill these roles by offering learning opportunities from each teacher, at the same time. For simultaneous instruction to work, teachers need to establish their roles, and identify who does what job.

Co-teachers need to establish their roles in three parts:

- Establish Parity (how both teachers demonstrate to students they are equal instructional partners and managers of the classroom)

- Establish Instructional Roles (how both teachers teach for most of the class at the same time)

- Establish Non-instructional Roles (how both teachers manage other aspects of instruction ex: data reporting, contacting parents, completing paperwork...)

## Parity

In the co-teaching classroom, "parity" is the act of establishing the co-teaching partnership. Each teacher must have a defined and equal status role. Teachers do NOT need to share in all aspects of instruction equally, but there must be a very solid understanding as to how that instruction will take place and each teacher's responsibility. To establish parity, co-teachers must first spend time asking each other important questions and discussing perspectives. If your teachers are using co-teaching as a way to share lost space due to over enrollment (example: two Kindergarten teachers in a very large classroom space, or an English teacher co-teaches with a Social Studies teacher for a double credit course called "American Studies."), then teaching roles are shared equally in many respects. The conversation between teachers is about curriculum and how teachers will accomplish curricular goals together.

If your teachers are providing co-teaching services as a way to have students have their special needs met (Special Education, English Language Services, Specialized Reading Services, Speech and Language...), then the goal in NOT to create two general education teachers. Both teachers need to understand curriculum and the obligations of meeting specialized plans (an IEP for example.) It is NOT the goal to have both teachers highly proficient in the curriculum, just as it would not be the goal to have both teachers be highly proficient in special education practices and the law. Administrators might hear something like: "I am not a specialist in the curriculum", or "I

# Classroom Roles

don't know the special practices related to the IEP." Both teachers have a professional obligation to have a solid understanding of each role and the requirements of that role, but we are not seeking a replicate skill set in both teachers (Kunkel, 2012).

For example/case study: The general education teacher (a mathematics teacher in 7th grade) is an expert in teaching math per the curriculum. The special education teacher knows there are 5 students in the classroom with IEPs in math calculation skills that are having difficulty with fractions. The special education teacher knows how to use a "Concrete, Representational, Abstract approach" to teaching the division of fractions using sticky notes instead of an algorithm. For the days lesson, the class is split into two groups. Group A, works with the general education teacher on the days lesson. Group B works with the specialist teacher on the hands on sticky note lesson (pre-teaching the fractions lesson with a hands-on approach). After 20 minutes, the groups switch teachers. Group B now works with the general education teacher and that teacher teaches the SAME lesson (differentiated) to Group B. Group A works with the specialist teacher that provides some extension or enrichment activities for the lesson. Both groups get the same lesson from the content specialist, AND a different lesson from the specialist teacher. The specialist teacher is able to work on the IEP needs of students, through specially designed instruction; while the content teacher ensures each group has had the content objectives as required.

From the example above, you can see that both teachers can have important roles in facilitating the learning, yet separate roles when it comes to delivering the curriculum. In parity conversations, it is important that each teacher discuss how they each contribute (differently) to students gaining access to the curriculum while meeting educational standards.

## Parity Discussion Points for Co-teachers

How will co-teachers...

- Provide physical references to both teachers? (names on the board, for example)

- Conduct conversations during instruction?

- Communicate with students?

- Communicate with each other?

- Manage disagreements with each other?

- Negotiate variances in classroom management styles?

# Co-Teaching for Administrators

- Capitalize on different instructional practices?
- Enforce differentiated assessment and grading practices?
- Decide the responsibility for the general education curriculum and the special education processes, procedures and paperwork?
- Use of materials and space?
- Create flexible groupings?
- Prepare and plan?
- Handle substitute teachers and or paraprofessionals?
- Communicate teaching preferences and styles with each other?
- Progress Monitor?
- Communicate with administration, counselors and other staff?

*"The ultimate criterion for success in teaching is - results!"*

*– James L. Mursell, "Successful Teaching," 1946, p. 1.*

## References

Kunkel, S. H. (2012). *Advancing Co-teaching Practices: Strategies for Success.* Cromwell, Connecticut: Kunkel Consulting Services.

Wiggins, G., & McTighe, J. (2007). *Schooling by Design.* Alexandria, Virginia: ASCD.

# Co-Teaching for Administrators

# Environment and Physical Arrangement

# 6

## Environment and Physical Arrangement

*Bert: I love to watch television. I love to watch TV in my old comfortable chair (Bert gets up to turn on the television)*

*Ernie enters: Hi ya, Bert! TV watching time huh?( Ernie sits in the chair.)*

*Bert: I always like to sit and watch my favorite TV show in that chair.*

*Ernie: Yeah, I know (remains seated in the chair.)*

*Bert: Can I sit in that chair?*

*Ernie: No, Bert, no chance. I am sitting here.*

*Bert: If that is the way you're going to be, then I just won't watch television. (Bert moves to TV and turns it off, exits)*

*Ernie: I can watch TV by myself. (Ernie gets up to turn the TV back on)*

*Bert enters: (sits in chair as soon as Ernie gets up.)*

**How should the classroom be set up?**
**How do co-teachers share the space?**

Sharing the physical space and using the physical space has great instructional impact. The use of the physical space demonstrates two important concepts: first - it is a demonstration of parity to the students; secondly- how space is used presets instruction for differentiated and small group arrangements. Wannarka and Ruhl reported "when the desired behaviour is interactive...like brainstorming or questioning the teacher, seating arrangements that facilitate interactions by proximity and position, such as clustered desks or semi-circles, should be utilised (Wannarka & Ruhl, 2008)."

In the white paper, *How Classroom Design Affects Student Engagement*, the SteelCase group reported:

"...Where physical space supports a focus on engaging experiences for students and faculty-have a significant effect on student engagement (Scott-Webber, Strickland, & Kapitula, 2015, p. 1)."

Their conclusions suggest: A large majority of students self-reported a moderate to exceptional increase in their engagement (84%), ability to achieve a higher grade (72%), motivation to attend class (72%) and ability to be creative (77%). Almost all faculty members reported a moderate to exceptional increase in student engagement (98%) (Scott-Webber et al., 2010, pp. 4-5).

Questions to consider about the importance of sharing space:

- Have teachers established two instructional spaces in the classroom, utilizing more than the front of the room where the instructional board is located? This is important for setting up instructional arrangements.

- Have teachers identified locations in the classroom for both teachers to have adequate storage for items such as instructional materials, personal items?

- Have teachers identified practices for moving the furniture to accommodate various arrangements?

- How is the movement to spaces within the classroom accomplished so instruction is not lost to disorganized transitions?

- Are teachers complaining about the lack of space?

- Do teachers remove some students from the classroom for space issues such as "it's too noisy"?

## Warning about Classroom Space!

It is not important that both teachers each have a separate desk or separate chair in the classroom. It is important that they have discussed and negotiated decisions together on how the furniture they do have is shared and used.

If one teacher always sits in the teacher chair in the front of the class and

# Environment and Physical Arrangement

one teacher always sits at a student desk, what non-verbal messages are communicated to students? For students that are represented by a specialist teacher, if their teacher is always in the "smaller" chair, how does that reflect on the students?

In conversation with students in co-taught classes, many of them have expressed they feel it is an "unfair" or an inequitable distribution in the classroom when one teacher seems to have a physically subordinate presence. One perceptive student said "When my special education teacher sits in the little chair, I think that represents how this school sees special education. It makes me feel we are less than equal." Another insightful student expressed "it is like being sent to the back of the bus."

## The Administrator's Role

When supporting and encouraging co-teaching pairs, observe how space is used and ask questions as to how they came to their decisions on the use of space. Facilitate discussions on the best use of space. Teachers need to create a plan to have flexible spaces that can accommodate a variety of instructional groupings for simultaneous instruction by both teachers. A movement away from whole group activities and plans for a variety of configurations is the ultimate goal.

Our mantra is "Rows Goes." If we examine how and why we use "rows" in education, it is a history in "because we have always done it that way" and not steeped in solid research-driven practices. Our "rows" in education are modeled from the history of schools in the United States initially being provided in old churches which were set up in rows. Our first school houses were created in rows. In modern times, our custodial staff might set up classrooms in rows and many teachers just use that configuration. Rows do not accommodate small group structures and are a barrier to best co-teaching practices.

## Strategies to Consider

- Guide co-teachers to pre-establish rules and routines to move quickly and efficiently into various groups. They should have physical desk and furniture arrangements to cluster students into two large groups in the classroom, three smaller groups, four small groups and six work groups. Ask teachers for their plans for these group sizes.

- Have teachers identify how they will teach from the various grouping spaces. If one teacher uses the electronic board in the front of the room, then the other teacher will use the white board in the back of the room. Have them brainstorm alternatives to needing a board (use of handheld white boards, flip charts, clipboards, sitting on the floor, standing stations, electronic sharing options...)

# Co-Teaching for Administrators

- Ask teachers to use rows for assessment times only. Challenge them to use cooperative and team building arrangements in the classroom that are flexible and varied.

- Create an opportunity for co-teaching teams to work together to "arrange" each other's classrooms and brainstorm creative use of space. This can be accomplished by have a "walk-through" after school whereby teachers creatively offer each other ideas on how to move desks and chairs and rearrange the classroom.

- Remind co-teachers they gain space when they group furniture together. Teachers often worry about not having enough space when rows are eliminated.

- Have teachers post pictures of instructional arrangement in the classroom. To save time and physical energy, teachers indicate the days arrangement and then students arrange the room per the chosen depiction. "Today we are learning in a three station rotation. Quickly move the desks to look like this picture…"

- Suggest co-teachers practice the various desk movements with students. If is often fun to "time" the movement of desks and have students "beat" their time or meet a time criteria.

- Encourage co-teachers to flexibly use space so that both teachers use both the front and the back of the room equally.

# Environment and Physical Arrangement

## Co-Teaching Configurations

The following graphic organizers show ten possible co-teaching configurations (Kunkel, 2012, pp. 62-64)

---

### Mirror
**(2 groups)**

Each teacher teaches the **same objective at the same time (groups do not switch)**

| Teacher 1 Group A | Teacher 2 Group B |

#### Variations
- **Vary** groups through the use of **Differentiation**
- Apply different **Teaching Styles**
- Each group offers different **Learning Styles** or **Multiple Intelligences** options
- Vary by using differentiated **Assessments**

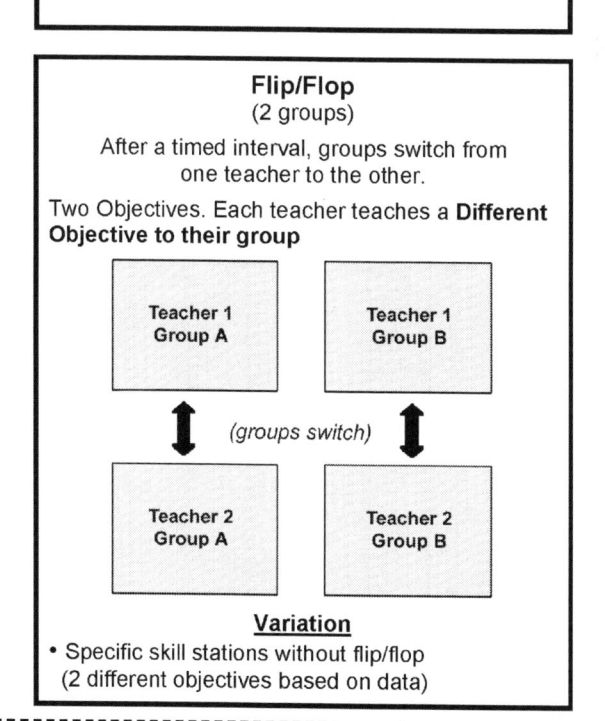

---

### Flip/Flop
**(2 groups)**

After a timed interval, groups switch from one teacher to the other.

Two Objectives. Each teacher teaches a **Different Objective to their group**

| Teacher 1 Group A | Teacher 1 Group B |

*(groups switch)*

| Teacher 2 Group A | Teacher 2 Group B |

#### Variation
- Specific skill stations without flip/flop (2 different objectives based on data)

# Co-Teaching for Administrators

**Flip/Flop Switch**
(2 groups)

Two or three teaching objectives

Data based groups. Teacher 1 teaches the main lesson, Teacher 2 PRE-teaches the lesson. After an interval, groups switch.

The pre-taught group then receives the same lesson from Teacher 1.

The lesson group receives RE-teaching or ENRICHMENT from Teacher 2.

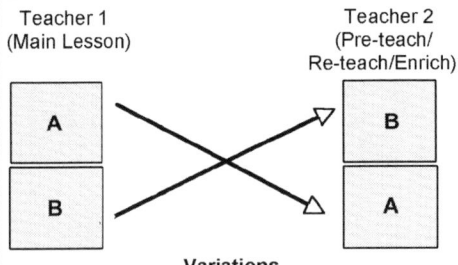

Teacher 1 (Main Lesson)     Teacher 2 (Pre-teach/Re-teach/Enrich)

```
   A  ──┐  ┌──  B
        ╲╱
        ╱╲
   B  ──┘  └──  A
```

**Variations**

- Each group receives initial pre-teaching lesson based on data-driven decisions.

- Students receive initial lesson (mirror style) then students are regrouped for re-teaching purposes.

---

**3 Station Rotation**
(3 groups: two teacher groups and one independent group)

Three teaching objectives

Each teacher instructs a group, and a third group completes an independent activity. After a timed interval, the groups switch. The students participate in all three groups.

*Note: In the independent group, students may work or sit: alone, in pairs, or as a group.*

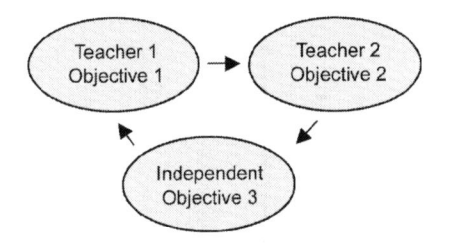

Teacher 1 / Objective 1 → Teacher 2 / Objective 2 → Independent / Objective 3 → (back to Teacher 1)

**Variations**

Three stations, but students only participate in two groups, with the following determined by the data:

- One teacher group and one independent group
- Two teacher groups, no independent group

# Environment and Physical Arrangement

## 3 Station Tiers
(3 groups: all teacher taught for some time)

One objective, tiered for maximum student success (NO Rotation)

Teacher 1 teaches the basic group (example: 20 minutes), Teacher 2 splits the same amount of time between the two other groups (example: 10 minutes teaching the intermediate group / then 10 minutes teaching the advanced group - teaching is alternated with independent work)

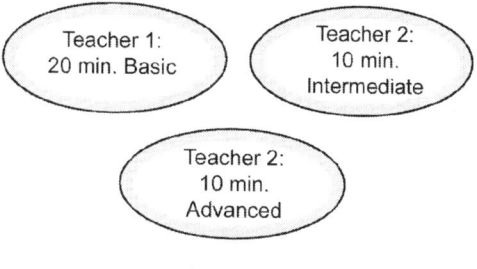

- Teacher 1: 20 min. Basic
- Teacher 2: 10 min. Intermediate
- Teacher 2: 10 min. Advanced

### Variation
- Teacher 1 spends 20 minutes enriching the advanced group and Teacher 2 spends 10 minutes teaching the other two groups.

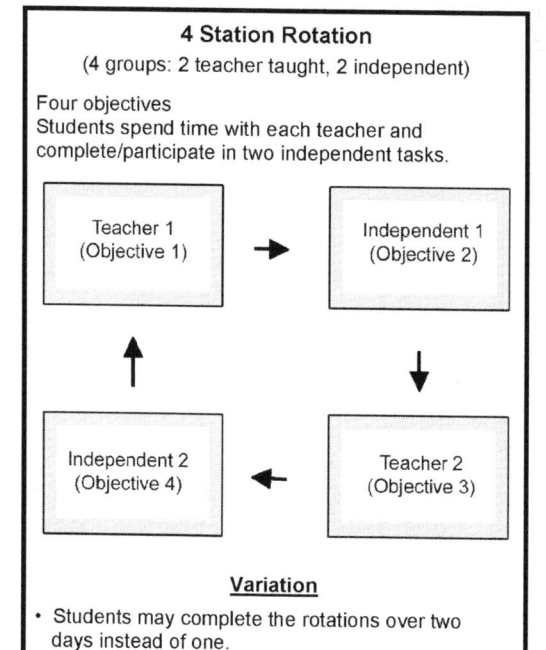

## 4 Station Rotation
(4 groups: 2 teacher taught, 2 independent)

Four objectives
Students spend time with each teacher and complete/participate in two independent tasks.

- Teacher 1 (Objective 1) → Independent 1 (Objective 2)
- ↓
- Teacher 2 (Objective 3) ← Independent 2 (Objective 4)
- ↑

### Variation
- Students may complete the rotations over two days instead of one.

# Co-Teaching for Administrators

## 4 Stations with one Teacher Flip/flop
(4 groups)

Two Objectives

The class is spit in half and each teacher alternates between an instructional group and an independent group. Students only see one teacher.

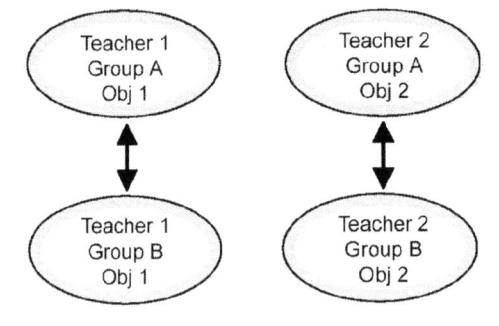

- Teacher 1 Group A Obj 1
- Teacher 2 Group A Obj 2
- Teacher 1 Group B Obj 1
- Teacher 2 Group B Obj 2

### Variations
- Teachers have the same objective for each group
- Teachers have different objectives for each group based on student needs.

## 4 Stations with Tiers
(4 groups)

One objective (NO rotation by students)

Each group works with a teacher for a specified amount of time, then the teacher moves to a second group. The lesson content is the same, but the lesson is differentiated for the various ability group levels.

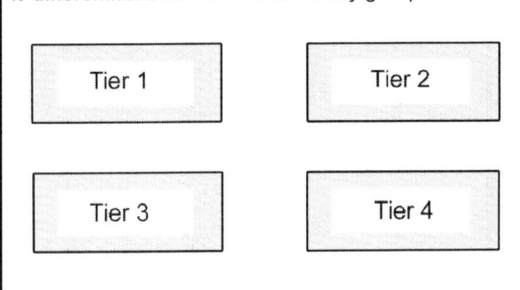

- Tier 1
- Tier 2
- Tier 3
- Tier 4

### Variation
- You may have one basic, two intermediate and one advanced group or any other ability combinations that make sense.

# Environment and Physical Arrangement

## 6 Stations with Interrupters
(6 groups)

Six Objectives

Students rotate between six groups. Two are teacher taught and four are independent. This configuration may take more than one class period if you do not work in a block schedule.

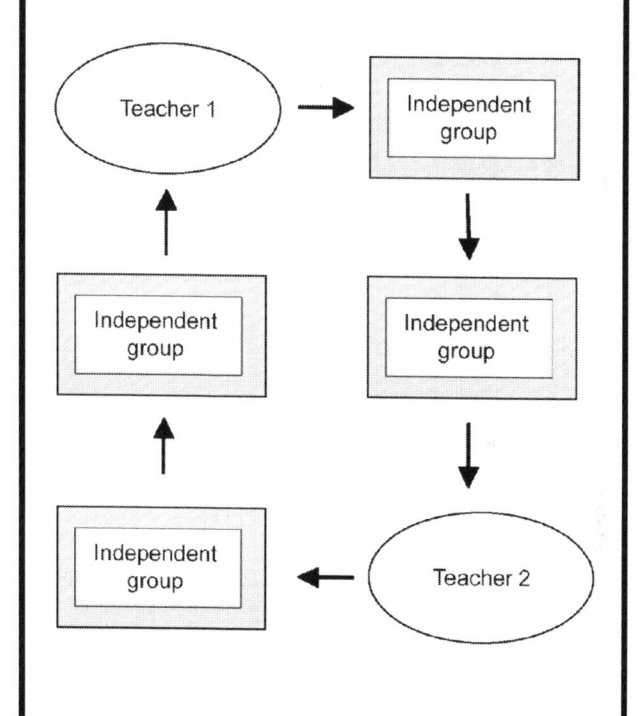

```
    Teacher 1    →    Independent
                        group
       ↑                   ↓
   Independent         Independent
     group               group
       ↑                   ↓
   Independent    ←     Teacher 2
     group
```

### Variations

- Students may double up in one group, or skip a group if it is appropriate.

# Co-Teaching for Administrators

**Skills Groups**
(1 large group task and
2 small flexible mini groups)

Objectives vary by group (many objectives: individualized)

Students are given a whole group task. Each teacher siphons off one to six students at a time to offer a short (in duration) mini lesson. Students are then returned to the group at large and another mini lesson group is created.

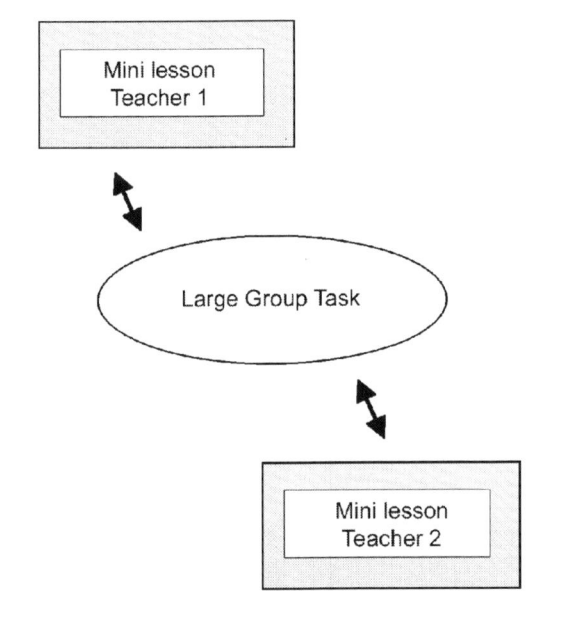

```
Mini lesson
Teacher 1
```

```
Large Group Task
```

```
Mini lesson
Teacher 2
```

**Variations**

- The purpose of the group may include re-teaching, pre-teaching, conferencing, assessment, skill focus, collaboration, drill, behavioral practice or any other need, as determined by the teachers. Each group has its own purpose, make-up and duration.

*"If real learning is to take place, our classrooms must be dependent on the collaboration of its learners, and not solely on the knowledge of its teachers."*

*– Robert John Meehan*

# Environment and Physical Arrangement

**References**

Kunkel, S. H. (2012). *Advancing Co-teaching Practices: Strategies for Success.* Cromwell, Connecticut: Kunkel Consulting Services.

Scott-Webber, L., Strickland, A., & Kapitula, L. R. (2015). *How Classroom Design Affects Student Engagement* [White paper]. Retrieved from https://www.steelcase.com/content/uploads/2015/03/Post-Occupancy-Whitepaper_FINAL.pdf.

Wannarka, R., & Ruhl, K. (2008) *Seating Arrangements that promote positive academic and behavioral outcomes: a review of empirical research.* Support for Learning, 23(2).

# Co-Teaching for Administrators

# 7

## Planning Instruction and Small, Flexible Groupings

*"Alone we can do so little. Together we can do so much".*

*– Helen Keller*

### Flexible Grouping Defined

As a strategy that can literally be "flexed" as needed, the use of flexible groups in inclusive co-taught classrooms can serve students with a range of abilities and can easily be adjusted to fit the many instructional needs and purposes of any classroom and/or lesson.

To begin, flexible grouping can be defined as basic strategy for differentiated instruction that allows students to work together in a variety of ways. It can be whole class, small groups, or even partners. In the context of this chapter, student groups may include representation from general education, special education, English Language Learners, and at risk students. Further, groups may be homogeneous (students at similar achievement levels) or heterogeneous (students at a wide range of achievement levels (Vaughn, Bos, & Schumm, 2014, p. 310). The time frame for flexible grouping can also vary depending upon the content that needs to be covered. For example, time frames may range from a single class period to an extended amount of time such as a week or even a month. Important to remember is that flexible groups are not permanent and can be changed according to student needs and instructional requirements.

A word of caution: Nierengarten suggests that "when collaborative classes exist in a school there is a temptation to overload these classes with high risk students because there are two teachers in the room ... as class rosters are prepared it is important to keep the principle of natural proportions in mind. ...Refers to the maintenance of the percentage of students with disabilities in the classroom that is represented by the school (Nierengarten, 2014, p. 76)." For example, If the number of students with IEPs are 10% of the school

# Co-Teaching for Administrators

population then the class should only have 10% of students with disabilities in the co-teaching environment. It is important to recognize that over assigning any one "category" of students to a group can create academic and even managerial issues. This must be weighed against the needs of students and the availability of your human resources. This is not a suggestion for practice. Use common sense. Meet student needs in the most professional and appropriate way possible.

## General Guidelines for Creating and Managing Flexible Groups in a Co-Taught Classroom

Before creating flexible groups for a short or long term unit of instruction, there are some general guidelines that should be considered. The first and most important to consider is: What is the expected learning outcome of the activity and what is the best type of grouping to meet these outcome? For example, considerations must include; the size of the group, homogeneous or heterogeneous, teacher or student lead, etc. Once a selection has been determined, there are several other issues which co-teachers should consider including:

- Assessment data of student strengths as well as needs must be examined before student group assignments are made.

- Learning styles of students.

- Student background knowledge of the subject area.

- Student personalities (knowledge of how students work and what placements may not be beneficial for individuals is critical as behavioral issues may result from improper placement).

- Motivational levels of students and interest levels in the subject area/topic.

- Consideration of "over assigning" students to the same group as previously mentioned (Marzano, Pickering, & Pollack, 2001) (We are LEADERS - Literacy Educators Assessing and Developing Early Reading Success, 2016).

It is also important to note that flexible grouping is exactly that, changes to the group makeup may need to be made once the instruction begins as issues may arise which require this. EVERY EFFORT should also be made to VARY group makeup as much as possible so that students do not become too "familiar" with their group. This may lead to individual students carrying the "load" of the group or other students not participating fully in the group.

Moving from creating groups to managing groups, several key points

# Planning Instruction and Small, Flexible Groupings

should be noted:

- Teachers must establish rules and procedures for group work. Care should also be taken to ensure that rules should be understood by all. (Written directions would greatly assist in this aspect). In the case of co-teachers, these rules must be mutually agreed upon.

- Students must receive explicit directions that clearly state the tasks that the group must complete.

- An established time limit must be set for group work. Students must be aware of when the group's work must be completed (Ex: a class period or a longer time such as over several class sessions).

- Co-teachers must be responsible for the management of group activities such as supervision of individual groups, checking for progress, and enforcing group rules.

## Benefits of Flexible Grouping

Flexible grouping when done properly and with sufficient planning, can have many benefits in any classroom but particularly an inclusive one with a co-teaching component such as we are discussing. Some of the primary ones include but are certainly not limited to the following:

- Insures all learners feel part of the community.

- Enables students to work cooperatively with peers.

- Enables co-teachers to share strategies as they develop group tasks and supervise and monitor groups in the process.

- Helps the majority of students by both learning to use time and using time effectively.

- Provides for individual differences for all.

- Meets academic, emotional, and social needs of each student.

- Students learn to work independently and cooperatively.

- Provides instructional scaffolding.

- Affirms student diversity.

- Facilitates student discussion.

- Capitalizes on student interests.

# Co-Teaching for Administrators

- Can facilitate peer mentoring.
- Provides experience working with different people.
- Promotes on task behavior.
- Helps students feel involved in the learning process (Marzano et al., 2001) (Valentino, 2000).

This brief chapter has presented just a few of the many possibilities of arranging, using, and benefiting from the use of flexible groups in the inclusive classroom. One of the many advantages of this differentiated instructional strategy in a co-teaching situation is that students and teachers will both benefit from the division of "labor" and the sharing of the results when the groups report their conclusions. Everyone wins and more importantly, learns!

*"Most great learning happens in groups. Collaboration is the stuff of growth."*

*– Sir Ken Robinson, Ph.D.*

## References

Marzano, R., Pickering, D., & Pollack, J. (2001). *Classroom Instruction that Works."* Alexandria, Virginia: ASCD.

Nierengarten, G. (2013). *Supporting Co-Teaching Teams in High School: Twenty research-based Practices.* American Secondary Education, 42(1), p. 76.

Valentino, C. (2000). *Flexible Grouping.* Retrieved from https://www.eduplace.com/science/profdev/articles/valentino.html

Vaughn, S., Bos, C., & Schumm, J. (2014). *Teaching Students Who Are Exceptional, Diverse and At Risk in the General Education Classroom.* Boston, Massachusetts: Pearson, p. 310.

*We are LEADERS - Literacy Educators Assessing and Developing Early Reading Success.* Retrieved from http://education.pitt.edu/EducationalResources/Teachers/LEADERS.aspx

# Co-Teaching for Administrators

# 8

## Guiding Evidence-Based Practices and Facilitating Planning, Assessment, and Progress Monitoring

*"For me at age 11, I had a pair of binoculars and looked up to the moon, and the moon wasn't just bigger, it was better. There were mountains and valleys and craters and shadows. And it came alive."*

*– Neil deGrasse Tyson*

Keeping abreast of the changes in special education has become an overwhelming job for special education teachers, special education and school administrators. This chapter outlines what administrators must do in order to guarantee that their co-teaching pairs are delivering instruction that truly meets the needs of all their students. When co-teaching is used for very specific purposes, like delivering special education, teachers must be able to design instruction and implement supports as well as specially designed instruction for students with IEPs. As part of the process the teachers must be able to collect individual data as well as group data that provides evidence of student learning outcomes. The school administrator must provide supports to teachers in the way of time to plan, evaluate and revise based on the data that the teachers have collected. The other overwhelming part of this tall order is to understand and know what evidence based practices are. Not too big an order is it?

Let's start by defining evidence-based practice and why it has become so important to special education. There are many different terms for evidence-based practices. According to the *IRIS Evidence-Based Practices Module (Part 1): Identifying and Selecting a Practice or Program* evidence-based practices are:

> ...skills, techniques, and strategies that have been proved to work through experimental research studies or large-scale research field studies (Evidence-Based Practices, 2016).

# Co-Teaching for Administrators

So why is this important? Well, IDEA 2004 reauthorization made it part of the law in Section §1400E

> *"...supporting high-quality, intensive pre-service preparation and professional development for all personnel who work with children with disabilities in order to ensure that such personnel have the skills and knowledge necessary to improve the academic achievement and functional performance of children with disabilities, including the use of scientifically based instructional practices, to the maximum extent possible (Individuals with Disabilities in Education Act, 2004);"*

Now this seems easy right? All we have to do is go to the encyclopedia of evidence based practices and pick the one that we want to try, right? Unfortunately it is not as easy as it seems.

Many principals, curriculum specialists and teachers are bombarded with literature from curriculum publishers advertising their "evidence based curriculum. If the literature that is sent outs out delivers on the promises that they extol we wouldn't have the education problems that seem to still plague our country. Unfortunately publishers have discovered the term "evidence based" and they use it quite liberally even if there is not significant proof that the program has not scientific evidence to support its effectiveness.

According to the IRIS module identifies reasons why it is difficult to identify evidence based practices.

- There are few opportunities for educators to learn about evidence based practices

- Specific information about evidence based practices can be difficult to locate

- Evidence-based practices are often presented in formats that educators find difficult to understand and to apply in the classroom

- Training on how to read and interpret researching findings is often inadequate

- Written descriptions might claim that practices and programs are evidence-based even though they are not backed by rigorous research.

- The criteria for deeming a practice or program "evidence-based" might vary depending on the organization or agency producing the effectiveness rating

- Many different terms used for evidence-based. You might see it as research-based, scientifically based, etc (Evidence-Based Practices,

## Guiding Evidence-Based Practices and Planning, Assessment, and Progress Monitoring

2016).

There are several federally funded government sites that you can go to for guidance.

### *What Works Clearinghouse*

ies.ed.gov/ncee/wwc

### *Intervention Central*

www.interventioncentral.org

### *Florida Center for Reading Research*

The Florida Center for Reading Research is a multidisciplinary research center at Florida State University that was established in 2002 by the Governor's office and Legislature.

www.fcrr.org

### *Premier Resources for Positive Behavior Interventions and Supports*

www.pbis.org

One of the problems of many websites have is that funding for the sites have been cut and therefore do not exist anymore.

Time must be given to teachers to identify, research, and discuss different evidence based practices that they feel might work for a particular student. So teachers may identify an evidence based practice that seems interesting they then must also look at the different populations it has been used with.

# Co-Teaching for Administrators

If the student the teacher wishes to use the practice with does not match the characteristics of the population that served as the sample then perhaps that practice should not be selected.

For example, a teacher has three students who are both English language learners and have IEPs. She wants to find a reading strategy that she feels she can use with these three students. The strategy that she has chosen to use has excellent evidence supporting its success with students who have reading problems but when she looks at the sample of students that it has been researched she sees that there are a few English Language Learners in the sample.

Is this a practice that she should use? This is a decision that she has to make based on the available research.

Another problem that may arise is that there has not been enough research done on a practice and it may be identified as a promising practice. The teachers must use their judgment if this is a practice that they want to try. Once they have decided to try a practice they must then collect data (progress monitor) to its effectiveness. If the IEP team has done their homework they may have identified a practice that they feel will work with the student but the teacher must still collect the data to see if the practice is working. In most cases the process will not be as onerous as this example. If there is more than one student with an IEP in the class the process must be implemented for each student. One practice is not going to work for all students. School districts must make sure that they are not using one practice for all students even though many IEPs I have seen have the same accommodations listed for many students.

So you can see that planning time must be allocated for your co-teaching teams.

## References

The IRIS Center, Peabody College Vanderbilt University. (2016). *Evidence-Based Practices (Part 1): Identifying and Selecting a Practice or Program.* Retrieved from *https://iris.peabody.vanderbilt.edu/module/ebp_01*

Individuals with Disabilities in Education Act of 2004, §1400E, 2004.

# Co-Teaching for Administrators

# Supervision and Evaluation of Co-Teachers

# 9

## Supervision and Evaluation of Co-Teachers

*"Politeness is the poison of collaboration."*

*– Edwin Land*

### What happens next?

Thus far, we have examined the steps necessary to establish a collaborative classroom environment that supports co-teaching and seeks to establish cooperative relationships with all the necessary stakeholders in such a venture. But before we examine the important question of how an administrator can best evaluate a co-teaching model to determine if it is truly functioning as it is expected to be, it is important to recap the changes the newly enacted ESSA (Every Student Succeeds Act) has on the teaching process as it relates to special education students. Administrators and teachers must be fully aware of the services they are to provide for students who are eligible for such under the provisions of this Act.

### ESSA Background

The passage of the Every Student Succeeds Act (ESSA) in December, 2015, rolled back some of the federal government's positions on education policy and created an opportunity for the individual states to more fully reflect on their systems of education, in terms of what is working well, what needs to be fixed, and perhaps what yet needs to be created.

Information provided in this section concerning changes and/or additions as to how the ESSA now applies to students who have been identified as requiring special services through the implementation of IEPs, has been obtained from a variety of resources including: The Council of Chief State School Officers (CCSSO), the Association for Supervision and Curriculum Development (ASCD), and Education Week.

# Co-Teaching for Administrators

## ESSA Changes that Concern Special Education

Although ESSA encompasses a wide range of topics and sub-topics, the brief information provided here relates to a selected few and how they apply to special education students in an inclusive environment including the co-teaching classrooms we have addressed thus far.

Standards: ESSA requires assurance that states adopt challenging academic content standards in reading, math, and science with three levels of achievement that are aligned with entrance requirements for credit-bearing coursework in the states' higher education system as well as the state's career and technical education standards. Further it allows states to develop alternate academic achievement standards for students with the most significant cognitive disabilities using a documented and validated standards-setting process.

ESSA also requires the same academic content and achievement standards for all students (except those with the most significant cognitive disabilities). This also means that these alternate achievement standards must be:

- Aligned with the state's challenging standards;

- Promote access to general education curriculum, consistent with the IDEA;

- Reflect professional judgment as to the highest possible standards achievable by the affected students;

- Designated in the IEP program developed for each student as the academic achievement standards that will be used for the student; and

- Aligned to ensure that a student who meets the alternate academic achievement standards is on track to pursue postsecondary education or employment (ESSA: Key Provisions and Implications for Students with Disabilities, 2016).

The application of this requirement is one that co-teachers working in an inclusive environment must provide for in their instructional planning and teaching, and include in their evaluation of student progress.

## Assessments

ESSA requires states to provide reasonable accommodations for students with disabilities. It also allows states to administer alternate tests for students with the most significant cognitive disabilities; however, these alternate tests may be used by NO MORE than 1% of the total number of students being assessed.

# Supervision and Evaluation of Co-Teachers

According to CCSSO, "there continue to be individuals who believe that students with disabilities cannot achieve rigorous standards or demonstrate mastery of such. As a result, there can be pressure not to include some students with disabilities in general assessments and push them towards an alternate assessment" (ESSA: Key Provisions and Implications for Students with Disabilities, 2016).

ESSA also requires that assessments are developed to the extent practicable, using the principles of Universal Design for Learning (UDL). As defined, UDL means a scientifically valid framework for guiding educational practice that:

- Provides flexibility in the ways information is presented, in the ways students respond or demonstrate knowledge and skills, and in the ways students are engaged; and

- Reduces barriers in instruction, provides appropriate accommodations, supports, and challenges, and maintains high achievement expectations for all students, including students with disabilities and students who are limited English proficient (ESSA: Key Provisions and Implications for Students with Disabilities, 2016, p. 4).

## Accommodations

ESSA requires that appropriate accommodations must be provided for students with disabilities identified under the IDEA Act, as well as those who are provided accommodations under acts other than IDEA.

## Interim Progress

According to ESSA, states must establish ambitious long-term goals with measures if interim progress for all students and separately for each subgroup of students including students with disabilities. Long-term goals must include at a minimum, improvement in academic achievement (as measured by proficiency on annual assessments as set by the state), and improved high school graduation rates. CCSSO states that "these provisions afford an opportunity for special education staff and others with experience working with students with disabilities, to inform conversations and influence decisions around the establishment of ambitious long-term goals and measures of interim progress (ESSA: Key Provisions and Implications for Students with Disabilities, 2016, p. 8). "

## Supervision and Evaluation of Co-Teachers

The brief overview of some of the provisions of ESSA provided a glimpse of those areas that must be considered when planning and implementing instruction in any inclusive classroom including the co-teaching model we are examining. But for our purposes, in moving forward, we must now

# Co-Teaching for Administrators

examine the important question of how an administrator can best evaluate a co-teaching model to determine if it is truly functioning as it is expected to be. In order to do this, let's take a quick look at some of the problems that a supervising administrator may face in evaluating a classroom taught by co-teachers.

## Problems Facing Supervising Administrators

Kamens, Susko, and Elliot conducted a study of New Jersey educators in which they explored administrator knowledge and practices as they related to the supervision and evaluation of co-teachers in inclusive classrooms. They found that there was "considerable inconsistency in administrator knowledge and practices and that professional development for administrators is warranted (Kamens, Susko, & Elliot, 2013, p. 166)." Clear themes emerged through their research that centered on three primary areas:

- Preparation and training related to co-teaching and inclusive practices: There was no consistent content to process by which administrators received knowledge or skills related to facilitating the co-teaching model as it relates to special education inclusive classrooms.

- Expectations and perspectives of co-teaching and inclusive practice: Although there was a general expectation that co-teachers should work together and share responsibility for planning, instruction, grading, and parent contact, expectations of such varied at elementary vs. secondary classrooms. Additionally, there was inconsistency among administrators concerning knowledge of co-teaching models, pairing of co-teachers, and roles of the general education vs. special education teacher.

- Challenges of supervising, supporting, and evaluating co-teachers: Administrators reported difficulty in defining support for co-teachers, and inconsistencies in observing co-teachers. These ranged from some evaluating co-teachers separately or together (Kamens et al. 2013, p. 186).

The challenges described by Kamens et al. center on providing co-teaching supervising administrators with clear and defined professional development on the intricacies of inclusive practices or specifically co-teaching, for without this background knowledge, there can be no meaningful evaluation. Moving from the required background knowledge necessary for administrators previous to conducting evaluations of co-teachers, Murawski and Lochner explain the necessary elements that they purport are required for effective co-teaching, thus providing some suggested areas of focus for the observing administrator. Co-teaching according to the authors, "requires three components: co-planning, co-instructing, and co-assessing (Murawski &

Lochner, 2011, p. 175)."

- Co-Planning: In true co-planning, teachers use their expertise in content area, differentiation, accommodations, positive behavior support, and pedagogy. Evidence to support co-planning can be obtained through examination of lesson, plans, modified material, and parent letters to list a few.

- Co-Instructing: Co-teachers engage students actively, use a variety of co-teaching approaches to regroup students, collect and share assessment information to better individualize, and are willing to try new things. Observers should look for behavior documentation, evidence of tiered lessons, accommodated assignments and tests, and joint grade books.

- Co-Assessing: Co-teachers should be able to describe or demonstrate ways in which they accommodate, provide alternative assessments, and treat students as individuals in determining their mastery of content. Observers should examine a variety of assessments that can validate accommodations and co-teachers should also demonstrate that they worked jointly on creating the assessments (Murawski & Lochner, 2011, p. 177).

## Observing Co-teaching Inclusive Classrooms

As noted, there are considerable issues that must be considered even before an administrator conducts an observation/evaluation of a co-teaching inclusive classroom. We have barely scratched the surface of these pre-observation issues. It is critical that administrators keep these background issues in mind and do their utmost to address any personal knowledge gaps.

But at this time, let us begin to examine some actual observation frameworks whereby we can then add some specific suggestions for observing and evaluating co-teachers in an inclusive classroom. We can start with one of the more recognized and used frameworks- the Danielson model. Charlotte Danielson's "Framework for Teaching" has been used as the basis for numerous state observation and evaluation tools. The use of the Danielson model's four main components can be adapted to fit the observation of a co-teaching classroom as we will see. For our purposes, all of the examples used will apply to both the general education and special education teachers in the inclusive classroom (Danielson, 2007, pp.3-4).

1. **Domain 1: Planning and Preparation**

    - Demonstrating Knowledge of Content and Pedagogy: This should include assessing the content knowledge of both teachers and how it is demonstrated through the related pedagogy.

# Co-Teaching for Administrators

- Demonstrating Knowledge of Students: This should include demonstration of both teachers regarding their knowledge of the learning process and child development, student skills and background knowledge, student interests, and of particular importance- student special needs.

- Setting Instructional Outcomes: This should include sequence of instruction, clarity of presentation, and suitability of lessons for diverse learners.

- Demonstrating Knowledge of Resources: This should include knowledge of resources (for teachers and students) for all levels of learning within the classroom.

- Designing Coherent Instruction: This should include design of all learning activities which includes lesson and unit structure, materials and resources and development of student groups.

- Designing Student Assessments: This should include alignment with learning outcomes and specific assessments designed for accommodations to meet individual student needs.

2. **Domain 2: The Classroom Environment**

- Creating an Environment of Respect and Rapport: This should include observing teacher interactions with all students and student-student interactions.

- Establishing a Culture for Learning: This should include evidence of teachers fostering pride in student work and achievement, and setting high learning expectations for all students.

- Managing Classroom Procedures and Managing Student Behavior: This should include observation of the management of student groups, transition time, managing materials and supplies and supervising other people in the classroom such as paraprofessionals. This should also include how student behavior is managed and how both teachers minimize disruptions due to student behavior issues.

- Organization of Physical Space: This is essential in a co-teaching environment. Safety and accessibility is foremost but ample space for small and large group instruction, stations, independent work areas, etc. should also be considered when evaluating this area.

3. **Domain 3: Instruction**

- Communicating with Students: This should include assessment of

## Supervision and Evaluation of Co-Teachers

how teacher directions and procedures are given, how explanations of content are provided, and the use of all written and oral language.

- Using Questioning and Discussion Techniques: This should include assessment of not only the quality of questions, but also what discussion techniques are used and how all students are actively engaged in the lesson.

- Engaging Students in Learning: This is the core of this area- how are activities and assignments designed to meet all levels of need, how are groups designed/changed, what materials/resources are available for the use of all students, and how is the structure and pacing of the lesson designed to meet all students.

- Using Assessment in Instruction: This should include examination of what the assessment criteria are, how diverse student needs are met in varying assessments for the same content areas, how student progress is monitored, and how feedback is given to students.

- Demonstrating Flexibility and Responsiveness: This area is also critical for co-teaching as both teachers should demonstrate flexibility in designing and adjusting lessons to meet student needs and responding to students as appropriate.

**4. Domain 4: Professionalism**

- This area encompasses a more "individualized" look at each teacher's professional demeanor in areas such as participation in professional community, professional growth and development, and demonstration of professional behavior. There are some areas that would apply more fully to the co-teaching classroom such as maintaining accurate records and communicating with families. These two areas should be a collaborative effort, where both teachers collaborate in grading students and both share in the communications with families. Important here is the need for families to be aware of what the co-teaching classroom looks like and how both professionals are involved in their child's learning environment. Ideally this should not be separated into "general" education and "special education" students where each teacher deals exclusively with one or the other.

# Co-Teaching for Administrators

## Other Suggestions for Observing Co-teachers in Inclusive Classrooms

Murawski and Lochner offer the following as a "Co-teaching Checklist":

- ☐ Two or more professionals working together in the same physical space.
- ☐ Class environment demonstrates parity and collaboration.
- ☐ Both teachers begin and end class together and remain in room the entire time.
- ☐ During instruction, both assist students with and without disabilities.
- ☐ Class moves smoothly with evidence of co-planning and communication.
- ☐ Differentiated strategies are used to meet the range of learning needs.
- ☐ A variety of instructional approaches are used including regrouping of students.
- ☐ Both teachers engage in appropriate behavior management as needed and are consistent in approach to behavior management.
- ☐ Difficult to tell the special educator from the general educator.
- ☐ Difficult to tell the special education students from the regular education students (Murawski & Lochner, 2011, p. 181).

Further the authors suggest the following to "listen for" in the co-teaching inclusive classroom:

- Co-teachers use language that demonstrates true collaboration and shared responsibility.

- Co-teachers phrase questions/statements so that it is obvious that all students in the class are included.

- Students' conversations evidence a sense of community (including peers with and without disabilities).

- Co-teachers ask questions at a variety of levels to meet all student needs (basic recall to higher order thinking).

Finally, co-author Sonya Heineman Kunkel, formulated a three stage co-teaching developmental self-assessment rubric which contains eight instructional components designed to assist co-teachers from those in the beginning stage (Stage/Level 1) through the Transition Stage (Stage 2)

## Supervision and Evaluation of Co-Teachers

to those who have reached the experienced stage (Stage 3/Level 2). And while the rubric was designed for use of self-assessment by co-teachers, administrators evaluating the co-teaching classroom can benefit by reflecting on the eight components and observing to what extent they exist in the co-teaching classroom. Further, artifacts such as lesson and unit plans, resource materials, assessments, student records, parent communication logs, should be evaluated by the supervising administrator with an eye for evidence of collaborative efforts (Kunkel, 2012, pp. 22-26).

Following is a chart reflecting the eight instructional components:

| Component | Definition | Evidence? |
|---|---|---|
| **Communication** | Use of verbal, non-verbal and social skills | Both teachers interacting with all students? Collaborative effort to communicate regarding adult needs as well? |
| **Physical Arrangement** | Placement and arrangement of materials, students, and teachers. | Does physical arrangement reflect an equally shared classroom? (Example: Two spaces from which to instruct) |
| **Instructional Presentation** | Presentations of lessons and structuring of classroom activities. | Evidence of equal responsibility in presenting content to all students? Evidence of varied styles of presentation that reflect each teacher's individual style of teaching? |
| **Classroom Management** | Rules, routines, consistent expectations, community and relationship building. | Evidence that both teachers have established and are "on the same page" regarding rules, routines, and expectations? Are students aware of this? |

# Co-Teaching for Administrators

| Component | Definition | Evidence? |
|---|---|---|
| **Curriculum Familiarity** | Competence and confidence with general education curriculum by both teachers. | Evidence that both teachers are comfortable in their knowledge of the taught curriculum? Do both carry the "instructional load"? |
| **Curriculum Goals/ Accommodations/ Modifications/ Specially-Designed Instruction** | Planning for specific IEP goals, objectives, accommodations and modifications. | Evidence that both teachers participated and shared in setting all components? Evidence that both teachers are thoroughly familiar with all student needs and adaptations as required? |
| **Instructional Planning** | Involves on-the-spot, day- to day, week-to week, and unit-to unit planning of coursework. | Evidence of both short and long term planning by both teachers? |
| **Assessment/Data/ Progress Monitoring** | Developing systems of evaluation, adjusting standards and expectations, maintaining course integrity, using data to improve learning conditions and opportunities. | Evidence that both teachers share equally in assessment of all students? In adjusting pacing as required? Evidence that data is used by both teachers to drive instructional goals and achievement? Evidence that both teachers examine data from assessments to monitor student progress, adjust instruction, and target learning needs? |

**References**

Danielson, C. (2007). *Enhancing Professional Practice, A Framework for Teaching.* Alexandria, Virginia: ASCD.

*ESSA: Key Provisions and Implications for Students with Disabilities.* (2016). Council of Chief State School Officers. Retrieved from http://www.ccsso.org/Documents/2016/ESSA/ESSA_Key_Provisions_Implications_for_SWD.pdf

Kamens, M., Susko, J., & Elliot, J. (2013). *Evaluation and Supervision of Co-Teaching: A Study of Administrator Practices in New Jersey.* NASSP Bulletin, 97(2)

Kunkel, S. H. (2012). *Advancing Co-teaching Practices: Strategies for Success.* Cromwell, Connecticut: Kunkel Consulting Services.

Murawski, W., & Lochner, W. (2011). *Observing Co-Teaching: What to Ask for, Look For, and Listen For.* Intervention in School and Clinic, 46(3). pp. 174-183.

# Co-Teaching for Administrators

# For Consideration

# 10

## For Consideration

While the following guiding suggestions/questions are not meant to be an all-inclusive *how-to* list of things to consider and do when establishing an effective co-teaching environment, it is nevertheless, our pick of the most important considerations when starting such an important endeavor.

### Develop a Collaborative Infrastructure

- ☐ District leaders including the superintendent, principal, and key stakeholders have developed a vision of embracing a school-wide inclusive program.

- ☐ District leaders, including the superintendent, principal, and key stakeholders have shared the vision with the entire school community. Parents should be included.

### Get the Right People on the Bus

- ☐ The leadership team has a clear picture of what needs to be accomplished including professional development.

- ☐ The leadership team has provided the tools to develop a culture of collaboration including:

    - ☐ Joint problem solving

    - ☐ Data sharing and analysis

    - ☐ Shared decision making

    - ☐ Distributed leadership

# Co-Teaching for Administrators

## Determining Best Practices

When choosing students best suited for a co-teaching environment the leadership team must consider:

- ☐ Students' need for specific instructional strategies (pre-planned)
- ☐ Students' needs for behavioral supports
- ☐ Students' needs for social opportunities
- ☐ Students' needs for skill development and practice

## Scheduling and Other Logistics

When determining co-teachers' schedules the leadership team must consider:

- ☐ How much time the co-teachers will teach together
- ☐ How much common planning time should be allotted
- ☐ What creative scheduling options have been considered

## Classroom Roles

When considering the individual roles of the teachers in a co-teaching classroom, teachers need to:

- ☐ Establish parity
- ☐ Establish instructional roles
- ☐ Establish non-instructional roles

## Environment and Physical Arrangement

When determining class-room setup in a co-teaching classroom, teachers need to:

- ☐ Establish two instructional spaces
- ☐ Identify storage locations for both teachers
- ☐ Identify procedures for seating arrangements
- ☐ Arrange room for transition movement

*For Consideration*

## Planning Instruction and Small, Flexible Groupings

When determining flexible groups of students, co-teachers need to consider students':

- ☐ Strengths and needs
- ☐ Learning styles
- ☐ Background knowledge
- ☐ Motivational and interest levels

## Guiding Evidence-Based Practices and Planning, Assessment, and Progress Monitoring

Have co-teachers...

- ☐ Examined evidence based practices?
- ☐ Selected those that they feel will meet the needs of their students?
- ☐ Collected and reviewed individual student assessment data through progress monitoring?
- ☐ Adjusted interventions needed based on data?

## Supervision and Evaluation

When supervising and evaluating co-teachers, administrators must consider evidence of:

- ☐ Co-planning
- ☐ Co-instructing
- ☐ Co-assessing

# CREC Educational Resources

To meet your needs, CREC offers educational resources in both print and digital media, including books, reference guides, manuals, e-books, webinars, and online professional development.

Resources are available on the following topics:

- Children's books
- Early childhood
- Educating struggling learners
- Leadership
- Literacy
- Numeracy
- Paraeducators
- School climate
- School management
- Special education

For more information about CREC's educational resources, visit www.crec.org/store, or scan the QR code.

CREC
Excellence in Education

Tom Sullivan
CREC Publishing Services
tosullivan@crec.org
860-240-6625

Made in the USA
Middletown, DE
06 June 2018